from SEA TO SHINING SEA

Mississippi

By Dennis Brindell Fradin and Judith Bloom Fradin

CONSULTANTS

David Sansing, Jr., M.S., History/Government Teacher,
Pearl High School, Pearl, Mississippi

Robert L. Hillerich, Ph.D., Professor Emeritus, Bowling Green State University;
Consultant, Pinellas County Schools, Florida

CHILDRENS PRESS®
CHICAGO

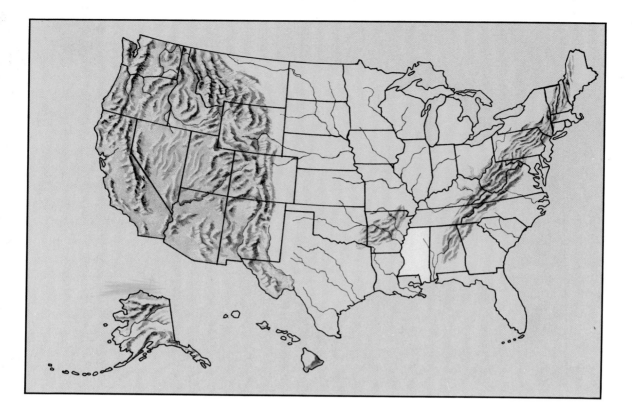

Mississippi is one of the fourteen states in the region called the South. The other southern states are Alabama, Arkansas, Delaware, Florida, Georgia, Kentucky, Louisiana, Maryland, North Carolina, South Carolina, Tennessee, Virginia, and West Virginia.

For our dear friend, Helen Handler, with love

Front cover picture: Stanton Hall, Natchez; page 1: A Biloxi marina; back cover: Mississippi Delta rice fields

Project Editor: Joan Downing
Design Director: Karen Kohn
Typesetting: Graphic Connections, Inc.
Engraving: Liberty Photoengraving

Library of Congress Cataloging-in-Publication Data

Fradin, Dennis B.
  Mississippi/ by Dennis Brindell Fradin & Judith Bloom
Fradin.
    p.   cm. — (From sea to shining sea)
  Includes index.
    ISBN 0-516-03824-9
  1. Mississippi—Juvenile literature. I. Fradin, Judith Bloom
II. Title. III. Series: Fradin, Dennis B. From sea to
shining sea.
F341.3.F7   1995   95-2695
976.2—dc20   CIP
                                                               AC

Table of Contents

Introducing the Magnolia State 4

From the Gulf Coast to the Delta. 7

From Ancient Times Until Today 13

Mississippians and Their Work. 27

A Tour of the Magnolia State 31

A Gallery of Famous Mississippians 45

Did You Know? 54

Mississippi Information 56

Mississippi History 58

Map of Mississippi. 60

Glossary 61

Index. 63

A Mississippi Choctaw girl dressed for the Choctaw Indian Fair

Introducing the Magnolia State

Mississippi lies in the Deep South. The state was named for the Mississippi River. This river forms most of the state's western border. *Mississippi* is an Indian name. It means "Great Water." Magnolia blossoms help make Mississippi smell sweet and look lovely. Mississippi is nicknamed the "Magnolia State."

Mississippi has a long history. Early Indians built huge mounds along the Mississippi River. A key Civil War battle took place at Vicksburg. A century later, Mississippi became a center in the fight for the rights of black people.

Today, Mississippi is a leading grower of cotton and rice. Packaged food is the state's top product. Tourism has become an important Mississippi business. Visitors enjoy the state's Gulf Coast beaches and history-filled places.

The Magnolia State is special in other ways, too. Where was the first state college for women opened? In what state was the first heart transplant performed? Where was Muppets-creator Jim Henson born? The answer to these questions is: Mississippi!

A picture map of Mississippi

Overleaf: The Pearl River Game Management Area

5

From the Gulf Coast to the Delta

From the Gulf Coast to the Delta

Mississippi covers nearly 48,000 square miles. Four of the thirteen other southern states border Mississippi. Alabama is to the east. Tennessee is to the north. Arkansas lies to the west. Louisiana is to the west and southwest. The Gulf of Mexico splashes Mississippi to the southeast. This strip of land is called the Gulf Coast.

Mississippi's land is made up of plains. These are rather flat lands with rolling hills. The plains along the Mississippi River are called the Delta. The Delta has some of the country's richest soil. Mississippi has no mountains. The state's highest point is Woodall Mountain. It is really a large hill. It stands 806 feet above sea level. The state's lowest point is sea level along the Gulf Coast. Several islands along the coast are part of Mississippi. They include Ship, Cat, and Horn islands.

Waters, Woods, and Wildlife

The country's longest river wiggles down Mississippi's western edge. Many other rivers criss-

Biloxi's beautiful beach stretches for miles along the Gulf.

The Mississippi River is 2,340 miles long. It begins in Minnesota and empties into the Gulf of Mexico off Louisiana.

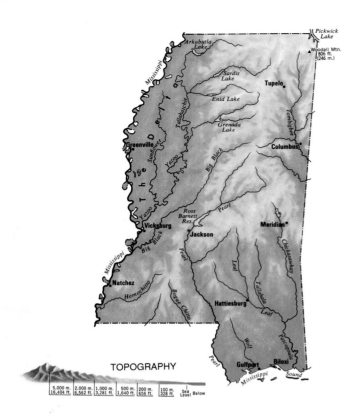

TOPOGRAPHY

5,000 m. | 2,000 m. | 1,000 m. | 500 m. | 200 m. | 100 m. | Sea
16,404 ft. | 6,562 ft. | 3,281 ft. | 1,640 ft. | 656 ft. | 328 ft. | Level | Below

Right: A bald cypress swamp on the Natchez Trace

cross Mississippi. They include the Tallahatchie, Yazoo, Big Black, Pearl, Chickasawhay, and Pascagoula.

Mississippi has several lakes. Its oxbow lakes formed when the Mississippi River changed course. Some oxbow lakes are Washington, Moon, and Beulah. The state's largest lakes were formed by damming rivers. A few of those lakes are Grenada, Arkabutla, and Ross Barnett.

One-eighth of Mississippi is wetlands. Much of this marshy land is near the Gulf Coast. Bayous flow through the wetlands. These are shallow, slow-moving waters. They link lakes with Delta rivers.

8

Over one-half of Mississippi is forested. The Piney Woods cover much of southern Mississippi. Many kinds of pine trees grow there. Bald cypresses and tupelo trees grow in Mississippi wetlands. Oaks, hickories, and sweet gums are other Mississippi trees. The magnolia is the state tree. The magnolia blossom is the state flower. Azaleas, camellias, and violets are other flowers found in the Magnolia State.

The bottle-nosed dolphin is the state water mammal. These dolphins swim along the Gulf Coast. Whales and sea turtles are also found in

Bottle-nosed dolphin

Green sea turtle

Alligator

Armadillos

coastal waters. Alligators crawl through Mississippi wetlands. Armadillos also live in Mississippi. Water moccasins are among Mississippi's snakes. The mockingbird is the state bird. It copies other birds' songs. The wood duck is the state waterfowl. Male wood ducks are red, yellow, white, purple, blue, and green. They are North America's most colorful ducks.

CLIMATE

Because it is so far south, Mississippi has much hot weather. Some inland places feel 90-degree-Fahrenheit temperatures about 100 days a year. The Gulf of Mexico cools the coast. Yet, even there, temperatures hit 90 degrees Fahrenheit about 55 days a year. On many winter days, temperatures top 55 degrees Fahrenheit in Mississippi. Some Mississippi towns have never had a below-zero-Fahrenheit temperature.

The Gulf Coast receives about 65 inches of rain a year. Other parts of the state receive about 50 inches a year. Sometimes heavy rainfalls cause the Mississippi and other rivers to flood. Snow sometimes falls on northern Mississippi. However, it usually doesn't amount to much.

Several tornadoes touch down in Mississippi each year. These are mighty, whirling windstorms. One hit Natchez in 1840. The Great Natchez Tornado killed more than 300 people. Hurricanes sometimes smack the Gulf Coast. These giant windstorms come off the ocean. In 1969, Hurricane Camille hit the coast. Its huge waves and 200-mile-per-hour winds caused hundreds of deaths and destruction to property along the Mississippi Gulf Coast.

A wild clover field

Overleaf: The Mississippi Memorial at Vicksburg National Military Park

11

From Ancient Times Until Today

FROM ANCIENT TIMES UNTIL TODAY

Millions of years ago, ocean waters covered Mississippi. Sharks' teeth have been found in many places. Basilosaurus bones have been found, too. They came from an ancient whale.

AMERICAN INDIANS

Emerald Mound

Buffalo roamed through Mississippi until the 1700s.

Ancient Indians reached Mississippi at least 12,000 years ago. They traveled about hunting. About 1,000 years ago, Mississippi's Indians began building huge mounds. Houses and temples stood atop some mounds. Certain mounds near the Mississippi River were "safety islands." People climbed up on them during floods.

By the 1500s, three major groups of Indians lived in Mississippi. They were the Chickasaw, Choctaw, and Natchez. Smaller groups included the Biloxi, Pascagoula, and Yazoo. These American Indians built wood cabins. They speared fish in Mississippi's rivers. They grew corn, pumpkins, and beans in Mississippi's rich soil. They also hunted deer, bear, and buffalo.

Europeans in Mississippi

Hernando De Soto was the first known European explorer in Mississippi. This Spaniard arrived in 1540. De Soto was the first European to see the Mississippi River. La Salle, a French explorer, traveled down the Mississippi River in 1682. He claimed the Mississippi Valley for France. This included present-day Mississippi.

La Salle paved the way for France to settle Mississippi. Pierre Le Moyne began Mississippi's first French settlement in 1699. It started as Fort

René-Robert Cavelier, Sieur de La Salle (center), claimed the Mississippi Valley for France on April 9, 1682.

Pierre and Jean Baptiste Le Moyne were brothers. Jean also founded Biloxi, Mississippi, in 1717 and New Orleans, Louisiana, in 1718.

A citizen in the costume of a French soldier at a festival in Gulfport

Maurepas on the Gulf Coast. Ocean Springs now stands there. Jean Baptiste Le Moyne, Sieur de Bienville, built Fort Rosalie in 1716. It grew into the town of Natchez. French colonists arrived and grew tobacco, rice, and indigo. A blue dye was made from indigo. In 1719, the French brought the first black slaves to Mississippi. The slaves worked in the colonists' fields.

France's hold on Mississippi was weak. At Natchez, the Natchez Indians rose up against the French in 1729. The next year, the French destroyed most of the Natchez. In 1736, the Chickasaws defeated the French in northeast Mississippi. English soldiers helped the Chickasaws.

By this time, there were thirteen English colonies along the Atlantic Ocean. England also claimed land up to the Mississippi River. In 1754, England and France went to war over this American land. In Mississippi, the Choctaws helped the French. The Chickasaws aided England. England won the war in 1763. French land east of the Mississippi River came under English rule. Land in Mississippi was granted to English people. Many were retired army and navy officers. But the number of settlers in Mississippi remained small under England.

Mississippi Becomes Part of the United States

The thirteen colonies declared their freedom from England in 1776. After the Revolutionary War (1775-1783), the colonies were called the United States. The new country gained England's land east of the Mississippi River. This included most of Mississippi. Spain had taken Mississippi's Gulf Coast. In 1798, the United States Congress made Mississippi a territory. In 1812, the Gulf Coast became part of the Mississippi Territory, too.

Thousands of Americans came to Mississippi. They farmed its rich land. By 1800, cotton was Mississippi's major crop. People called the crop "King Cotton." In the early 1800s, a road called the Natchez Trace was started. It linked Natchez, Mississippi, with Nashville, Tennessee. The trace followed a path first used by buffalo and then by Indians. Today, a highway follows the old trail. It is called the Natchez Trace Parkway.

By 1817, Mississippi's population was about 60,000. That December 10, Congress made Mississippi the twentieth state. David Holmes was Mississippi's first governor. Jackson has been the capital since 1822.

A section of the Natchez Trace near Port Gibson

Trace is an old word for path or road.

A painting of field slaves at work on a Mississippi River cotton plantation

Over half of all Mississippi farmers owned no slaves in 1860.

THE CIVIL WAR

Cotton continued to gain in importance. More slaves were brought in to grow it. By 1860, the state's black slaves outnumbered white people 437,000 to 354,000. Many slaves worked on huge farms called plantations. On some plantations, fifty or more slaves did the work.

Slavery had been outlawed in the North. In 1860, Abraham Lincoln was elected president of the United States. He was from Illinois, a northern state. Many southerners feared he would end slavery in the South. Eleven southern states seceded (withdrew) from the United States. They declared themselves the Confederate States of America. Mississippi seceded on January 9, 1861. Mississippian Jefferson Davis became the Confederacy's first and only president.

From 1861 to 1865, the Confederacy (South) and Union (North) fought the Civil War. Mississippi sent more than 78,000 men to fight for the Confederacy. The Battle of Vicksburg in Mississippi was a turning point of the war. For forty-seven days, Union forces hammered away at this

The Union attack at Vicksburg

General Braxton Bragg was military adviser to Confederate President Jefferson Davis.

Mississippi River town. The Confederates fought back. Both sides suffered many deaths. Food became scarce in Vicksburg. Townspeople dug caves to escape the shelling. Finally, the Confederates surrendered the city on July 4, 1863. This Union victory gave the North control of the Mississippi River. Two years later the war ended.

Mississippi had suffered terribly from the war. About 36,000 of its soldiers had died. Thousands more returned home missing an arm or a leg. Farm animals had been taken by Union soldiers. Towns and railroads had been damaged.

With the war's end, the United States government freed the slaves. It also gave black men the right to vote. Until 1870, United States soldiers stayed in Mississippi. They protected the newly freed black people. Mississippi had to prove that it would obey United States laws. In December 1869, Mississippians passed a new constitution. It, too, granted black people the right to vote. On February 23, 1870, Mississippi was allowed to return to the Union.

For a time, black Mississippians voted. Some served in government. Hiram Rhoades Revels was appointed to the United States Senate in January 1870. Revels was the country's first black senator

(1870-1871). He was a minister from North Carolina. Blanche K. Bruce became the first full-term black senator (1875-1881). He had been born a slave in Virginia.

In 1890, however, the white people of Mississippi wrote a new state constitution. It took the vote away from most black people. At that time, segregation became the rule in the South. Black people could not go to the same schools, hotels, or restaurants as white people. They had to use separate public bathrooms. Groups like the Ku Klux Klan attacked black people. Sometimes these hate groups lynched (hanged) black people.

Left: Senator Blanche K. Bruce
Right: Masked members of the Ku Klux Klan

Segregation *means keeping the races apart.*
Integration *means allowing people of different races to use the same place at the same time.*

World Wars, Depression, and Civil Rights

In 1917, the United States entered World War I (1914-1918). About 65,000 Mississippians served. One of the first military flight schools in the United States started in Mississippi. It was at Payne Field, outside of Columbus.

After the Civil War, many Mississippians suffered from poverty. Plantations had been broken up into smaller farms. Many Mississippians—blacks and whites—became sharecroppers. They farmed other people's land. They received a share of the value of the crops they raised. In years with poor harvests, sharecroppers ended up owing landowners. By the

These sharecroppers grew cotton in Hillhouse, Mississippi.

1920s, two-thirds of all Mississippi farmers worked other people's land. Mississippians made only one-third the income of the average American.

The Great Depression (1929-1939) made things even worse in Mississippi. The price of cotton fell from twenty cents a pound in the 1920s to five cents by 1931. Thousands of Mississippians lost their farms. One day in 1932, one-fourth of Mississippi's land was auctioned for unpaid taxes.

World War II (1939-1945) helped end the Great Depression. The United States entered the war in 1941. About 250,000 Mississippi men and women served in uniform. Vessels built by Ingalls Shipyard at Pascagoula also helped win the war.

James Meredith

The civil-rights movement grew after World War II. In 1954, the United States Supreme Court said that segregated public schools were unlawful. James Meredith enrolled at the University of Mississippi in 1962. He was the first black student ever to go there. In 1964, Mississippi's grade schools and high schools started to desegregate. Restaurants and other public places also became integrated.

The fight for blacks' voting rights was long and difficult. In 1963, Medgar Evers was shot to death in Jackson. He had been working for black

Mississippians' voting rights. Not until 1994 was his killer sentenced to life in prison. In 1964, three young civil-rights workers were murdered near Philadelphia, Mississippi. In 1965, the United States Congress passed the Voting Rights Act. About 130,000 Mississippians registered to vote. In 1969, Charles Evers was elected mayor of Fayette. He was Medgar's older brother. Charles Evers became the first black mayor of a racially mixed southern city.

CURRENT PROBLEMS AND FUTURE HOPES

The Magnolia State has overcome numerous obstacles in the last 100 years. Though one-third of Mississippians haven't finished high school, many improvements have been made in the state's educational system over the past ten years. Mississippi's per-person income is only $14,000 a year. One-fourth of all Mississippians live in poverty.

Mississippi's farmers have especially suffered. Machines replaced many farm workers in the 1950s and 1960s. From 1981 to 1990, the number of Mississippi farms fell from 56,000 to 40,000. Thousands of small farmers went out of business. Many were in the Delta. This is one of the country's poorest regions.

A floating casino in Vicksburg

Since the 1980s, Mississippians have turned to new industries. Catfish farming has boomed in the Delta. The fish are raised in ponds, much like a crop. This has created thousands of jobs. Furniture-making has become a giant Mississippi industry. So has gambling. In 1990, state lawmakers voted to allow dockside gambling. The floating casinos are found on the Gulf Coast and the Mississippi River. Gamblers have pumped billions of dollars into the state. More than 30,000 Mississippians work in this new industry. Tourism has also become a giant business. Money spent by visitors to Mississippi doubled between 1990 and 1994. Mississippians hope that growing industries will improve their way of life.

Overleaf: A student at Milsaps College, in Jackson

Mississippians and Their Work

MISSISSIPPIANS AND THEIR WORK

The population of the Magnolia State is almost 2.6 million. Thirty states have more people. Nineteen have fewer. More than half of all Mississippians live on farms or in small towns. Only three other states are also mostly rural. Of every 100 Mississippians, 63 are white and 36 are black. No other state has a higher rate of black people to white people. Only about 16,000 Hispanics and 13,000 Asians live in Mississippi. Almost 9,000 American Indians live in Mississippi. Most of them are Choctaw.

MISSISSIPPIANS AT WORK

Almost 1 million Mississippians have jobs. More than 250,000 of them make goods. Packaged foods are the state's top product. These include meats, milk, and baked goods. Mississippi is one of the top five shipbuilding states. It is also among the top ten logging states. Wood products include lumber, furniture, and paper. Many Mississippians also make clothes. They include work clothes, dresses, shirts, and slacks.

Mardi Gras in Biloxi

Girls in Native American dress take part in a Natchez powwow.

27

More than 210,000 Mississippians work for the government. Many serve at Keesler Air Force Base in Biloxi. Others test rockets at the Stennis Space Center north of Bay St. Louis. Still others work in Mississippi's many state parks.

About another 210,000 Mississippians sell goods. The products range from potato chips to cars and computers. Roughly 200,000 Mississippians provide services. They include doctors, nurses, lawyers, and hotel workers. Tourism is an important business in Mississippi. Hotels line the Gulf Coast. It is a popular vacationland because of the hot climate.

More than 50,000 Mississippians farm. Mississippi ranks fifth in the country at raising broiler chickens. It produces 300 million of them a year. That's more than one for every American. Broiler chickens are raised for their meat. Only Texas and California grow more cotton than Mississippi. Other important crops are rice, soybeans, peanuts, and pecans.

Catfish ponds have replaced cotton fields in the Mississippi Delta. Mississippi leads the country with farm-raised catfish. The state is also a leader at catching shrimp. Oysters and red snappers are other important catches.

Cotton being harvested in the Mississippi Delta

About 6,000 Mississippians work at mining. The state is a big oil and natural gas producer. Mississippi is a top miner of high-grade gravel. The Magnolia State also mines many kinds of clay. One of them is fireclay. This is used to make bricks for fireplaces and furnaces.

A Pascagoula commercial fisherman mending nets

Overleaf: An aerial view of Jackson

A Tour of the Magnolia State

A TOUR OF THE MAGNOLIA STATE

Mississippi has much for visitors to enjoy. Many sun and swim on the Gulf Coast beaches. Others tour Civil War battlefields and civil-rights landmarks. Beautiful old homes also attract visitors to Mississippi, especially in Natchez and Vicksburg.

THE GULF COAST

Pascagoula is near Mississippi's southeast corner. It is a good place to start a tour. The Old Spanish Fort is there. The fort is Mississippi's oldest building. It was built as a house by a French blacksmith in 1718. Later, the Spanish used it as a fort. It had very thick walls. The Scranton Floating Museum is also in Pascagoula. This 70-foot shrimp boat is docked on the Pascagoula River. On it, visitors can learn about Gulf Coast shrimping and wildlife.

Ocean Springs is west of Pascagoula. A replica of Pierre Le Moyne's Fort Maurepas is there. Many artists live in Ocean Springs. Walter Anderson (1903-1965) was one of them. He was known as the "South's Greatest Artist." Anderson would row

Walter Anderson's rowboat is one of the exhibits at the Walter Anderson Museum of Art in Ocean Springs.

to the nearby islands and stay for weeks to paint the beautiful Gulf Coast wildlife. From nearby Horn Island, Anderson painted animals, the sea, and wildflowers. The Walter Anderson Museum of Art displays many of his works.

Biloxi is west of Ocean Springs. Begun in 1717, Biloxi is now the state's second-largest city. Beauvoir was Confederate president Jefferson Davis's last home. Today. visitors can tour the house and library. Biloxi is well known for catching and canning shrimp. Visitors can learn about this at the Seafood Industry Museum.

Exterior and interior views of Beauvoir, the last home of Confederate president Jefferson Davis

Visitors listening to a guide at Fort Massachusetts

Gulfport is just west of Biloxi. This Gulf Coast city was begun as a railroad town in 1887. Gulfport is now the state's sixth-biggest city. Sea lions and dolphins perform at Gulfport's Marine Life Oceanarium.

Ship Island is off the coast. Ferry boats from Biloxi and Gulfport take visitors out to the island. They can view Fort Massachusetts. It was built on the island in 1858. Northerners seized the fort during the Civil War. They used it as a prison for southern soldiers.

Bay St. Louis is near the west edge of Mississippi's Gulf Coast. St. Augustine Seminary was founded there in 1923. It was a Catholic seminary for training black priests. America's first black Catholic bishop was appointed from there in 1965. His name was Father Harold Perry. Visitors enjoy the seminary's lovely grounds. A statue of Christ praying is in the seminary's man-made grotto.

People are trained to be priests or ministers at seminaries.

SOUTHERN MISSISSIPPI HIGHLIGHTS

Hattiesburg was founded in 1882. A rich lumberman named it for his wife, Hattie Hardy. Today, Hattiesburg is the state's fourth-biggest city. The All-American Rose Garden is in Hattiesburg. Nearly 1,000 rose bushes bloom from spring through fall. The University of Southern Mississippi is located in Hattiesburg.

Laurel is just north of Hattiesburg. Landrum's Homestead is there. It shows rural Mississippi life from the 1800s. Buildings there include a log cabin and a water-powered gristmill. The mill once ground corn into cornmeal.

Woodville is near the state's southwest corner. Nearby is the Clark Creek Nature Area. Seven waterfalls tumble over the bluffs there. The highest drops 50 feet. Trails wind through Clark Creek. Hikers may spot deer and armadillos. Also outside

Woodville is Rosemont Plantation. This was Jefferson Davis's boyhood home.

Natchez is to the north. Begun in 1716, it is the oldest city on the Mississippi River. Natchez is best known for its homes built before the Civil War. The Governor Holmes House dates from 1794. Auburn (1812), Rosalie (1820), Magnolia Hall (1858), and Longwood House (1860-61) are other beautiful Natchez homes.

Emerald Mound is northeast of Natchez. Early Mississippi Indians built the mound about 750 years ago. Temples stood upon it. Springfield Plantation is farther north. The plantation house was complet-

Natchez has more than 500 buildings, including homes, churches, banks, and stores, that were built before 1860. No other American city has as many.

Longwood House

ed in 1791. Reportedly, Andrew Jackson married Rachel Robards in the house that year. Jackson later served as president of the United States (1829-1837). The Ruins of Windsor are nearby. Windsor was built from 1859 to 1861 by 600 slaves. In 1890, the five-story house burned down. Twenty-three huge columns are all that remain of the house today.

Lorman is between Springfield Plantation and the Ruins of Windsor. Alcorn State University was founded there in 1871. It was the country's first state-supported college for black people. Alcorn's graduates include Charles and Medgar Evers.

Left: The Ruins of Windsor
Right: Springfield Plantation

The USS Cairo
Museum at Vicksburg
National Military Park

CENTRAL MISSISSIPPI

Vicksburg lies along the Mississippi River. It is north of Natchez. Vicksburg National Military Park almost circles the city. The park preserves the Civil War battlefield. Nine Confederate forts stand there. The USS *Cairo* Museum is part of the park. Confederates sank this Union gunboat in the Yazoo River in 1862. It was the first warship sunk by an electrically exploded mine. In 1964, the *Cairo* was raised for display.

The Biedenharn Coca-Cola Museum is in Vicksburg. Joseph Biedenharn bottled the first Coca-Cola in Vicksburg in 1894. Coca-Cola had been invented earlier in Georgia. The museum tells the story of this American soft drink.

Jackson is east of Vicksburg. The town began as a trading post in 1792. In 1821, the land was chosen to be Mississippi's capital. Today, Mississippi lawmakers meet in the State Capitol. This 1903 building was modeled after the United States Capitol in Washington, D.C. Jackson is also the state's biggest city. About 200,000 people live there.

Jackson has many fine museums. The Mississippi State Historical Museum features Indian beadwork and pioneer displays. The museum is in

No other Mississippi city has even one-fourth as many people as Jackson.

Interior and exterior views of the Mississippi State Capitol dome

the Old State Capitol. State lawmakers met there from 1839 to 1903. Jackson's Davis Planetarium is a good place to learn about astronomy. The Smith Robertson Museum traces the history of black Mississippians. The Mississippi Museum of Art has works from around the world. The Mississippi Museum of Natural Science is another Jackson museum. Children enjoy its aquarium filled with Mississippi fish.

Mississippi Petrified Forest is north of Jackson at Flora. Its giant petrified trees and logs date back 36 million years. Water once covered this woodland. Minerals in the water turned the wood to stone.

Meridian is east of Jackson. This is Mississippi's fifth-biggest city. The Jimmie Rodgers Museum is in Meridian's Highland Park. The "Father of Country Music" is honored in an old railroad depot. Before Rodgers wrote and sang songs, he worked for a railroad. The Dentzel Carousel is also in Highland Park. It has twenty-eight carved horses, deer, lions, and tigers. The carousel has delighted children since 1909.

The Choctaw Indian Reservation is northwest of Meridian. About 5,000 Choctaws live there. Each July they hold a fair. The Choctaws perform dances and play stickball. Nearby is Nanih Waiya

A social dance at a Choctaw Indian school

Mound. That is where the Choctaws believe their people came into being.

Columbus is north of the reservation. Mississippi University for Women was founded there in 1884. It was the country's first state-supported college for women. Friendship Cemetery is also in Columbus. Union and Confederate soldiers are buried there. On April 25, 1866, Columbus women placed flowers on the graves. This was Mississippi's first Memorial Day.

Greenwood is west of Columbus. It is a great cotton market. Farmers sell their cotton crop at Cotton Row. Greenwood's Cottonlandia Museum has exhibits on cotton growing. Florewood River Plantation is near Greenwood. It shows how a cotton plantation of the 1850s worked.

Greenville is west of Greenwood. It is the state's third-largest city. Greenville is also the state's largest Mississippi River port. It is in the Delta. Each fall, the city hosts the Delta Blues Festival. The Greenville Flood Museum tells about the 1927 Mississippi River flood. The town was under water for seventy days. Only Indian mounds stood above the water. Winterville Mounds is near Greenville. Thousands of Indians once lived there. They built the Great Temple mound and ten smaller ones.

Northern Mississippi

Cleveland is north of Greenville. Delta State University is there. The school's Museum of Natural History has many Indian arrowheads. Fossils can be seen there, too. They include 15,000-year-old mastodon bones.

Mastodons were somewhat like present-day elephants.

Clarksdale is north of Cleveland. The Delta Blues Museum is there. Visitors can learn about Mississippi's Delta blues musicians. They can also listen to blues recordings.

Oxford is in the middle of northern Mississippi. It is home to the University of Mississippi. Many Mississippi governors graduated from "Ole Miss." The school has more than 10,000 students. Rowan Oak is near the college. It was author William Faulkner's home. Faulkner wrote the outline for *A Fable* on his study wall. Visitors can still see the outline today.

William Faulkner won the 1955 Pulitzer Prize in literature for this novel.

Holly Springs is to the north. The Kate Freeman Clark Art Gallery is there. Clark was born in and grew up in Holly Springs. She painted landscapes and portraits. Her mother told her: "It would be like selling a child to sell one of your paintings!" Clark never allowed any of her works to be sold. The gallery houses more than 1,200 of her

paintings. No other place holds that many paintings by one artist.

Corinth is near Mississippi's northeast corner. The Battle of Corinth was fought there in October 1862. Today, visitors can walk across Battery Robinett. Union soldiers held this spot. In 1862, Corinth's Curlee House served as headquarters for four generals. They were Generals Braxton Bragg, Earl Van Dorn, John Hood, and Henry Halleck.

Tupelo is a good place to end a Mississippi tour. It is south of Corinth. This city was Elvis Presley's hometown. Visitors are welcome at the Elvis Presley Birthplace. Presley (1935-1977) lived in this two-room house during his first three years.

Left: The Lyceum is on the campus of the University of Mississippi in Oxford. Right: An interior view of Rowan Oak, the home of author William Faulkner

Halleck was a Union general. The other three men were Confederate generals.

Overleaf: Jefferson Davis

A Gallery
of Famous
Mississippians

A Gallery of Famous Mississippians

The Magnolia State has produced many famous people. They include authors, musicians, and political leaders.

Jefferson Davis (1808-1889) was born in Kentucky. His family moved to Mississippi in 1810. Davis is remembered as the president of the Confederacy. But earlier he represented Mississippi in the U.S. House of Representatives (1845-1846) and the Senate (1847-1851). He also served as U.S. secretary of war (1853-1857). After the Confederacy lost the Civil War, Davis spent two years in prison. He later wrote *The Rise and Fall of the Confederate Government* (1881).

Elizabeth Taylor Greenfield (about 1819-1876) was born a slave in Natchez. As a child, she was taken to Pennsylvania and freed. She lived with Mrs. Greenfield, a Quaker. Mrs. Greenfield encouraged Elizabeth's singing. Elizabeth became a world-famous concert singer. She was called the "Black Swan." **William Grant Still** (1895-1978) was born in Woodville. In 1930, he composed *Afro-American Symphony*. It was the first major symphony written by a black American. **Leontyne Price** was born in

Leontyne Price

Laurel in 1927. She decided to become a singer when she was nine. This famous black opera star has won thirteen Grammy Awards.

Blues music grew out of the work songs of black field hands. **"Mississippi" John Hurt** (1892-1966) was an early blues musician. Born near Greenwood, he became a singer. "Candy Man Blues" and "Avalon Blues" are among his recordings. **Howlin' Wolf** (1910-1976) was born Chester Arthur Burnett in West Point. He became a blues singer and guitarist. Howlin' Wolf helped start the Chicago style of blues. **Robert Johnson** (1911-1938) was born in Robinsville. He was known as "King of the Delta Blues." As a boy, Vicksburg-

Left: "Mississippi" John Hurt
Right: Elvis Presley

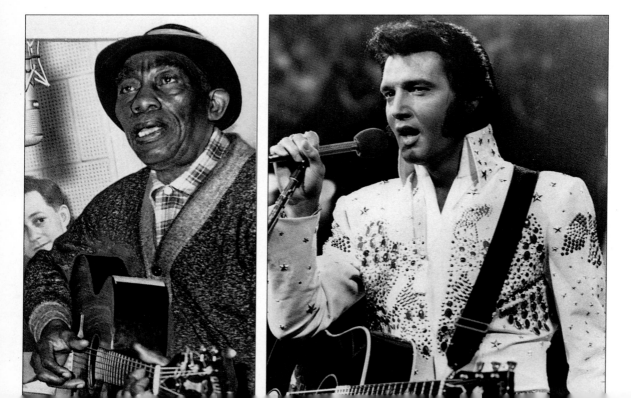

born **Willie Dixon** (1915-1922) spoke in rhymes. Later, he wrote more than 300 blues songs. "Little Red Rooster" is one of them. **Muddy Waters** (1915-1983) was born McKinley Morganfield in Rolling Fork. This sharecropper's son became a blues singer. Muddy Waters was the first to play the blues on the electric guitar. "Got My Mojo Working" was one of his songs. **Riley B. ("B. B.") King** also became a famous singer and electric-guitar player. King was born on a cotton plantation near Indianola in 1925. "B. B." stands for "Blues Boy." "Lucille" was a B. B. King hit.

Elvis Presley (1935-1977) was born in Tupelo. When he was about twelve, he was given a guitar.

From left to right: Blues musicians B. B. King, James Cotton, Muddy Waters

Muddy Waters is called the "Godfather of the Blues."

Elvis Presley's record sales, movies, and concerts earned $18 billion dollars during his lifetime.

47

Fannie Lou Hamer

Presley became the "King of Rock and Roll." His hits included "Heartbreak Hotel" and "Hound Dog." Presley also starred in *Love Me Tender* and many other movies.

Charlie Pride was born in Sledge in 1938. Pride bought his first guitar at age fourteen. He grew up to become the first black country music star. In 1980, Pride was named top male country artist of the decade.

Eliza Poitevent Holbrook Nicholson (1849-1896) was born in Pearlington, on the Pearl River. She became a poet known as **Pearl Rivers.** In 1876, Nicholson became one of the country's first female newspaper publishers. She built the New Orleans *Times-Picayune* into a fine paper. It is still printed today. Before leaving Mississippi, Nicholson had a small house on the Hobolochitto River. By 1904, a town had grown near her house. It was named Picayune after the newspaper.

Elizabeth Lee Hazen (1885-1975) was born at Rich. She taught high-school science in Jackson. At age forty-two, Hazen earned a doctorate in science. She and Rachel Brown discovered mystatin in 1948. This medicine cures fungus infections.

Fannie Lou Hamer (1917-1977) was born in Montgomery County. As a child, she picked cotton.

In 1963, Hamer registered to vote. She helped other black people register, too. Because of her civil-rights work, she was jailed and beaten. Hamer helped form the Mississippi Freedom Democratic Party. It fought racism in Mississippi.

Unita Blackwell was born in Lula in 1933. She also picked cotton as a child. Blackwell worked with Fannie Lou Hamer in the 1960s. In 1976, Blackwell became mayor of Mayersville. She was Mississippi's first black female mayor. Blackwell improved her town's housing and streets.

Many great writers have come from Mississippi. **William Faulkner** (1897-1962) was born in New

Twice, Unita Blackwell was president of the National Conference of Black Mayors.

William Faulkner and his wife Estelle in front of Rowan Oak, their home in Oxford

Albany. He lived most of his life in Oxford. Faulkner became a great writer. He set his stories in the South. Faulkner won the 1949 Nobel Prize for literature. *The Sound and the Fury* is one of his best-known works. **Eudora Welty** was born in Jackson in 1909. She also sets her stories in the South. Welty's novel *The Optimist's Daughter* won the 1973 Pulitzer Prize in literature. **Richard Wright** (1908-1960) was born near Natchez. He grew up in Jackson. Wright's *Black Boy* tells of his early life. *Native Son* is a story of poverty and crime.

Left: Tennessee Williams
Right: Richard Wright

The great playwright **Thomas Lanier (Tennessee) Williams** (1911-1983) was born in Columbus, Mississippi. His *Glass Menagerie* is often done by high school students. Two of his other plays won Pulitzer Prizes.

Children's author **Mildred Taylor** was born in Jackson in 1943. Taylor listened to her family's stories of life in the South. Later, she retold those stories in books. *Song of the Trees* was Taylor's first novel. *Roll of Thunder, Hear My Cry* won the 1977 Newbery Medal.

Jerry Clower was born in Liberty in 1926. He became a famous storyteller. Clower became known as the "Mouth of Mississippi." One Clower tale is "The Maddest Man I Ever Saw!" **James Earl Jones** was born in 1931 in Arkabutla. He overcame a childhood stutter and become a famous actor. Jones won a Tony Award for Best Actor in 1969. It was for his role in the play *The Great White Hope.* Jones was Darth Vader's voice in the *Star Wars* movies. *Field of Dreams* was a popular film in which he appeared.

James "Cool Papa" Bell (1903-1991) was born in Starkville. He starred in the Negro leagues. That was before the major leagues allowed black players. His lifetime batting average was an amazing

Once in a 200-game season "Cool Papa" Bell (above) stole 175 bases.

Walter Payton

Oprah Winfrey

.341. He was also a great base stealer. Bell was elected to the Baseball Hall of Fame in 1974.

Mississippians **Willie Brown** and **Walter Payton** made the Pro Football Hall of Fame. Brown was born in Yazoo City in 1940. He intercepted fifty-four passes in his career. Payton was born in Columbia in 1954. His playing days were all with the Chicago Bears. Payton holds the NFL record for yards rushing in a game—275. He also holds the career rushing record with 16,726 yards. **Jerry Rice** was born in Crawford in 1962. Rice plays for the San Francisco 49ers. In 1994, Rice set the NFL career record for touchdown pass catches.

Jim Henson (1936-1990) was born in Greenville. He grew up in Leland. There he caught frogs with his friend Kermit Scott. Henson became a puppeteer. He created the Sesame Street Muppets. Henson named Kermit the Frog for his childhood friend. Other Henson Muppets include Miss Piggy, Big Bird, Cookie Monster, and Oscar the Grouch.

Oprah Winfrey was born in Kosciusko in 1954. She became the youngest woman and first black newscaster on Nashville (Tennessee) television. Since 1985, she has hosted television's "The Oprah Winfrey Show." Winfrey reaches 15 million American viewers a day.

The birthplace of Oprah Winfrey, Jim Henson, "Cool Papa" Bell, and Kate Freeman Clark . . .

Home, too, of the Le Moyne brothers, Jefferson Davis, and Hiram Rhoades Revels . . .

A major producer of broiler chickens, cotton, rice, catfish, and shrimp . . .

A state that is world famous for its blues musicians and award-winning authors . . .

This is Mississippi—the Magnolia State.

Jim Henson is shown here with some of his famous Muppets.

Did You Know?

In 1900, Casey Jones drove the *Cannonball Express* on its run from Memphis, Tennessee, to Canton, Mississippi. Seeing that the track was blocked by another train at the town of Vaughan, Jones had the train's fireman jump. Jones stayed on board, slowing the train down, but not enough to avoid a crash. Jones was the only one who died in the crash. Since then, a song was written about Casey Jones. The Casey Jones Museum is in Vaughan.

Mississippi has many places named for groups of Indians. The state has Chickasaw and Choctaw counties. It also has towns named Natchez, Biloxi, Pascagoula, and Yazoo City.

Before it was called the "Magnolia State," Mississippi was nicknamed the "Bayou State."

Each September, Biloxi hosts a sand sculpture contest. Up to 100 five-member teams compete for about $4,000 in prizes.

The town of Midnight was named in an unusual way. One night in the 1880s, a group of hunters were playing cards by a campfire. One of the men had claimed the land they were on. He bet his land and lost. The winner checked his watch and said, "Well, boys, it's midnight, and that's what I'll call my land."

Petal, a town on the Leaf River, is home to the Checker Hall of Fame. Checker players from around the world go there for tournaments. The great checker player Charles Walker of Petal once played 306 people at one time. He won 300 games, tied 5, and lost just 1.

Hurricane Camille changed Mississippi's map in 1969. Hurricane-driven waters cut Ship Island in two. Now there are East Ship and West Ship islands. The gap between the islands was named "Camille Cut."

Edward Adolph Barq invented Barq's Root Beer in Biloxi in 1898.

Some Mississippi towns with unusual names include Alligator, Piggtown, Sunflower, Chunky, Hot Coffee, Money, and Jumpertown.

A Mississippi slave who ran away and joined the Union Army was said to be the last Civil War survivor. Sylvester Mack Magee was reportedly 130 years old when he died in 1971.

By 1989, Jim Henson's "Muppet Show" was the most-watched television show in the world, with 235 million viewers in 106 countries.

Laurel native Ralph Boston won the 1960 Olympic gold medal for the men's long jump. Willye White from Money won the 1956 Olympic silver medal for the women's long jump. Gunnison native Mildrette Netter was on the women's team that won the 1968 gold medal for the 400-meter relay race.

In 1957 near Enid Dam, Fred Bright caught the largest white crappie on record. The fish weighed over five pounds.

55

MISSISSIPPI INFORMATION

State flag

Magnolia tree

Magnolia blossom

Area: 47,716 square miles (the thirty-second biggest state)

Greatest Distance North to South: 340 miles

Greatest Distance East to West: 142 miles

Borders: Tennessee to the north; Alabama to the east; Arkansas and Louisiana to the west; Louisiana and the Gulf of Mexico to the south

Highest Point: Woodall Mountain, 806 feet above sea level

Lowest Point: Sea level, along the Gulf of Mexico

Hottest Recorded Temperature: 115° F. (at Holly Springs, on July 29, 1930)

Coldest Recorded Temperature: -19° F. (at Corinth, on January 30, 1966)

Statehood: The twentieth state, on December 10, 1817

Origin of Name: Mississippi was named for the Mississippi River; the name is an Indian word meaning "Great Water" or "Father of Waters"

Capital: Jackson (since 1822)

Earlier Capitals: Washington (1802-1817); Natchez (1817-1821); Columbia (1821-1822)

Counties: 82

United States Representatives: 5

State Senators: 52

State Representatives: 122

State Song: "Go Mississippi," by Houston Davis

State Motto: *Virtute et Armis* (Latin, meaning "By Valor and Arms")

Nicknames: "Magnolia State," "Eagle State," "Mud-cat State," "Bayou State"

State Seal: Adopted in 1817   **State Flag:** Adopted in 1894

State Tree: Magnolia **State Flower:** Magnolia blossom

State Bird: Mockingbird **State Waterfowl:** Wood duck

State Fish: Largemouth bass **State Insect:** Honeybee

State Fossil: Prehistoric whale **State Stone:** Petrified wood

State Shell: Oyster shell **State Beverage:** Milk

State Land Mammal: White-tailed deer

State Water Mammal: Bottle-nosed dolphin

State Butterfly: Spicebush swallowtail

Some Rivers: Mississippi, Tallahatchie, Yazoo, Big Black, Pearl, Chickasawhay, Leaf, Pascagoula, Tombigbee

Some Lakes: Grenada, Pickwick, Arkabutla, Sardis, Ross Barnett

Wildlife: White-tailed deer, armadillos, foxes, mink, woodchucks, rabbits, muskrats, raccoons, squirrels, alligators, bears, water moccasins and other snakes, mockingbirds, ducks, wild turkeys, sparrows, woodpeckers, pelicans, egrets, gulls, many other kinds of birds, bass, catfish, crappies, shrimp, oysters, crabs

Farm Products: Broiler chickens, eggs, beef and dairy cattle, milk, hogs, cotton, rice, soybeans, peanuts, pecans, watermelons, peaches, sweet potatoes, sorghum, wheat

Manufactured Products: Meats and other packaged foods, ships, furniture, paper products, electrical equipment, appliances, telephones, clothing, chemicals,

Mining Products: Oil, natural gas, sand and gravel, clays, crushed stone

Fishing Products: Catfish, shrimp, oysters, menhaden, red snappers

Population: 2,573,216, thirty-first among the fifty states (1990 U.S. Census Bureau figures)

Major Cities (1990 Census):

Jackson	196,637	Gulfport	40,775
Biloxi	46,319	Tupelo	30,685
Greenville	45,226	Pascagoula	25,899
Hattiesburg	41,882	Columbus	23,799
Meridian	41,036	Clinton	21,847

Mockingbird

Wood duck

Spicebush swallowtail butterfly

MISSISSIPPI HISTORY

LaSalle

De Soto

About 10,000 B.C.—The first people reach Mississippi

About A.D. 1000—Early Mississippi Indians begin building mounds

1540—Hernando De Soto, a Spanish explorer, reaches Mississippi

1682—French explorer René-Robert Cavelier, Sieur de La Salle, claims a huge area for France, including Mississippi

1699—Pierre Le Moyne, Sieur d'Iberville, begins Mississippi's first French settlement at what is now Ocean Springs

1716—Jean Baptiste Le Moyne, Sieur de Bienville, begins a second Mississippi settlement that becomes Natchez

1717—Jean Baptiste Le Moyne begins Biloxi

1719—The French bring the first black slaves into Mississippi

1763—England gains French land east of the Mississippi River, including Mississippi

1781—Spain claims Mississippi's Gulf Coast

1783—All of Mississippi, except the Gulf Coast, becomes part of the United States

1798—The U.S. Congress makes Mississippi a territory

1800—The territory's first newspaper, the *Mississippi Gazette,* is published at Natchez

1812—The Gulf Coast becomes part of the Mississippi Territory

1817—On December 10, Mississippi becomes the twentieth state

1840—The Great Natchez Tornado kills more than 300 people

1848—The University of Mississippi opens at Oxford

1861-65—During the Civil War, Mississippi sends more than 78,000 men to fight for the Confederacy

1863—The Confederates surrender Vicksburg after a forty-seven-day siege

1865—The war ends in a Union victory; the southern slaves are freed

1870—Mississippi rejoins the United States

1871—Alcorn State University is founded as the country's first state-supported college for black students

1884—Mississippi University for Women is established at Columbus as the country's first state-supported college for women

1890—Mississippi's new state constitution takes the vote away from most black people

1917-18—About 65,000 Mississippians help win World War I

1927—A huge Mississippi River flood forces about 200,000 people to leave the Delta area

1929-39—During the Great Depression, farming and manufacturing suffer in Mississippi

1941-45—Almost 250,000 Mississippi men and women help win World War II

1962—James Meredith becomes the University of Mississippi's first black student

1963—Black leader Medgar Evers is murdered in Jackson

1964—Three young civil-rights workers are murdered near Philadelphia, Mississippi; Mississippi's first public schools are integrated

1969—Charles Evers is elected mayor of Fayette; Hurricane Camille kills 256 people in Mississippi and nearby Louisiana

1985—The Tennessee-Tombigbee Waterway opens, which helps shipping through Mississippi

1987—Mike Espy becomes Mississippi's first black person in the U.S. House of Representatives since 1883

1988—Governor Ray Mabus signs a law to improve conditions in the Mississippi Delta, one of country's poorest areas

1990—The Magnolia State's population reaches 2,573,216

1992—Tornadoes hit Brandon and other parts of Mississippi, killing fifteen people and injuring about 300 people

MAP KEY

Ackerman	D6
Alligator	C3
Arkabutla	A4
Arkabutla Lake	A4
Bay St. Louis	K5
Benoit	D2
Big Black River	E4
Biloxi	K6
Brandon	F4
Canton	F4
Cat Island	K6
Chickasawhay River	H,I7
Choctaw Indian Reservation	F6
Chunky	F6
Clark Creek Nature Area	I2
Clarksdale	B3
Cleveland	C3
Clinton	F3
Columbia	I5
Columbus	D7
Corinth	A6
Crawford	D6
Emerald Mound	H2
Enid Dam	C4
Fayette	H2
Greenville	D2
Greenwood	D4
Grenada Lake	C5
Gulf of Mexico	K7
Gulfport	J6
Gunnison	C3
Hattiesburg	H5
Hobolochitto River	J5
Holly Springs	A5
Horn Island	K6,7
Hot Coffee	H5
Indianola	D3
Jackson	F4
Jumpertown	A6
Kosciusko	E5
Lake Beulah	C2
Lake Washington	E2
Laurel	H6
Leaf River	I6
Liberty	I3
Lorman	G2
Lula	B3
Mayersville	E2
Meridian	F6
Midnight	E3
Mississippi City	J6
Mississippi Petrified Forest	F3
Mississippi River	B3;G2
Money	D4
Moon Lake	B3
Myrtle	B6
Nanih Waiya Mound	F6
Natchez	H2
Natchez Trace Parkway	D5,6;G3
New Albany	B6
Ocean Springs	J6
Oxford	B5
Pascagoula	K7
Pascagoula River	J7
Pass Christian	J6
Pearlington	K5
Pearl River	E,F5;J4,5
Petal	H6
Philadelphia	E6
Picayune	J5
Pickwick Lake	A7
Piggtown	F5
Rich	B3
Robinsville	A4
Rolling Fork	E3
Rosemont Plantation	I2
Ross Barnett Reservoir	F4
Ruins of Windsor	G3
Sardis Lake	B4
Ship Island	K6
Sledge	B4
Springfield Plantation	H2
Starkville	D6
Sunflower	D3
Tallahatchie River	B4
Tennessee-Tombigbee Waterway	B,C7
Tombigbee River	C,D7
Tupelo	B6
Vaughan	E4
Vicksburg	F3
Washington	H2
West Point	D6
Winterville Mounds	D2
Woodall Mountain	A7
Woodville	I2
Yazoo City	E3
Yazoo River	F3

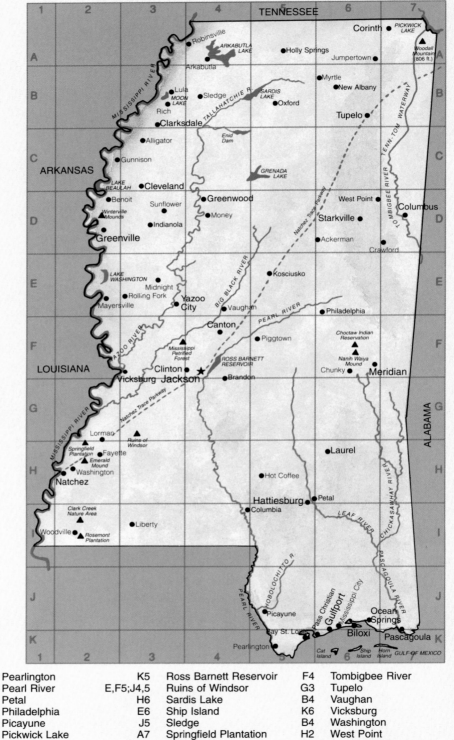

GLOSSARY

bayou: Slow-moving, often marshy water that links lakes with rivers and rivers with ocean waters

blues: A sad, moody kind of music based on the work songs of black field hands

capital: The city that is the seat of government

capitol: The building in which the government meets

century: A 100-year period

civil rights: The rights granted citizens of the United States by the Constitution

climate: The typical weather of a region

coast: The land along a large body of water

constitution: A written plan of government, explaining a state's laws

delta: Rich land formed by a river's flooding

explorer: A person who visits and studies unknown lands

fossil: Remains of animals or plants that lived long ago

hurricane: A huge storm that forms over the ocean

integration: The process of bringing people of different races together

million: A thousand thousand (1,000,000)

oxbow lake: A body of water, in the shape of an oxbow, that forms when a river changes its course

permanent: Lasting

plains: Flat lands

plantation: A large southern farm

population: The number of people in a place

reservation (Indian): Land in the United States that has been set aside for American Indians

rural: An area of small towns and farms

secede: To withdraw from or leave

segregation: The process of keeping the races apart

seminary: A place where priests or ministers receive training

sharecropper: A person who farms the land of another and receives a share of the value of the crops

slavery: A practice in which some people own other people

territory: The name of a part of the United States before it became a state

tornado: A powerful, whirling windstorm that comes from a funnel-shaped cloud

tourism: The business of providing such services as food and lodging for visitors

trace: An old word for a path or road

INDEX

Page numbers in boldface type indicate illustrations.

agriculture, 4, **11**, 16, 17, 18, **18**, 22-24, **22**, 28, **28**, 35, 41, 57, 59
All-American Rose Garden, 35
American Indians (Native Americans), **3**, 14, **14**, **15**, 16, 41, 58
Anderson, Walter, 32, 33
Arkabutla Lake, 8, 57
art, 32-33, **32**
Auburn, 36
Barq, Edward Adolph, 55
Bay St. Louis, 28, 34-35
Beauvoir, 33, **33**
Bell, James, 51-52, **51**
Beulah Lake, 8
Biedenharn, Joseph, 38-39
Big Black River, 8, 57
Biloxi, **7**, **27**, 28, 33, 34, 54, **54**, 57, 58
Biloxi people, 14
Blackwell, Unita, 49
borders, 7, 56
Boston, Ralph, 55
Bragg, Braxton, **20**, 43
Brandon, 59
Bright, Fred, 55
Brown, Willie, 52
Bruce, Blanche K., 21, **21**
Camille, Hurricane, 11, 55, 59
capital. *see* Jackson
Cat Island, 7
Checker Hall of Fame, 55
Chickasawhay River, 8, 57
Chickasaw people, 14, 16
Choctaw people, **3**, 14, 16, 27, 40-41, **40**
Chunky, 55
civil rights, 20-21, 23-24, 59
Civil War, 18-20, **19**, **20**, 34, 38, 41, 43, 55, 58
Clark, Kate, 42-43
Clark Creek, 35
Clarksdale, 42
Cleveland, 42
climate, 10-11, 55, 56, 58, 59

Clinton, 57
Clower, Jerry, 51
Columbia, 56
Columbus, 41, 57, 59
Corinth, 43
Cotton, James, **47**
Cottonlandia Museum, 41
Cotton Row, 41
Curlee House, 43
Davis, Houston, 56
Davis, Jefferson, 19, 33, 36, **44**, 45
Davis Planetarium, 40
Delta, 7, 24, 25, 41, 59
Dentzel Carousel, 40
De Soto, Hernando, 15, 58, **58**
Dixon, Willie, 47
economy, 22-23, 24
education, 23, 24, **26**, 34-35, 37, 41, 42, **43**, 58, 59
elevation, 7, 56
Emerald Mound, **14**, 36-37
employment, 27-29
English, 16-17, 58
Enid Dam, 55
Espy, Mike, 59
Evers, Charles, 24, 37, 59
Evers, Medgar, 23-24, 37, 59
Faulkner, William, 42, 49-50, **49**
Fayette, 24
fishing, 25, 28, **29**, 55, 57
Flora, 40
Florewood River Plantation, 41
forests, **8**, **9**
Fort Massachusetts, 34, **34**
Fort Maurepas, 15-16, 32
Fort Rosalie, 16
French, 15-16, **15**, 58
Friendship Cemetery, 41
geography, 7-10
government, 20, 21, 56, 59
Great Depression, 23, 59
Great Natchez Tornado, 11, 58
Great Temple mound, 41
Greenfield, Elizabeth Taylor, 45

Greenville, 41, 57
Greenwood, 41
Grenada Lake, 8, 57
Gulf Coast, 4, 7, **7**, 8, 9, **9**, 10, 11, 16, 17, 25, 28, 32-35, 58
Gulf of Mexico, 7, **7**-8, 10, 56
Gulfport, 34, 57
Halleck, Henry, 43, **43**
Hamer, Fannie Lou, 48-49, **48**
Hardy, Hattie, 35
Hattiesburg, 35, 57
Hazen, Elizabeth Lee, 48
Henson, Jim, 4, 52, **53**, 55
Highland Park, 40
history, 4, 14-25, 58-59
Holly Springs, 42
Holmes, David, 17
Holmes House, 36
Hood, John, 43
Horn Island, 7, 33
Hot Coffee, 55
Hurt, John, 46, **46**
industry, 25, 27, 57, 59
Jackson, 17, **30-31**, 39-40, 56, 57
Jackson, Andrew, 37
Johnson, Robert, 46
Jones, Casey, 54
Jones, James Earl, 51
Jumpertown, 55
Keesler Air Force Base, 28
King, Riley B., 47, **47**
Ku Klux Klan, 21, **21**
lakes, 8, 57
La Salle, René-Robert Cavelier, Sieur de, 15, **15**, 58
Landrum's Homestead, 35
Laurel, 35, 55
Leaf River, 55, 57
Le Moyne, Jean Baptiste, 58
Le Moyne, Pierre, 15, 32, 58
Lincoln, Abraham, 18-19
Longwood House, 36, **36**
Lorman, 37
Mabus, Ray, 59

Magee, Sylvester Mack, 55
Magnolia Hall, 36
maps of Mississippi showing:
  cities and geographical features, **60**
  location in U. S., **2**
  products and history, **5**
  topography, **8**
Mardi Gras, **27**
Marine Life Oceanarium, 34
Meredith, James, 23, **23,** 59
Meridian, 40, 57
Midnight, 54
mining, 29, 57
Mississippi, University of, 42, **43,** 58, 59
Mississippi Freedom Democratic Party, 49
Mississippi Indians, 36, 58
Mississippi Memorial, **12-13**
Mississippi Museum of Art, 40
Mississippi Museum of Natural Science, 40
Mississippi Petrified Forest, 40
Mississippi River, 4, **7-8,** 14, 15, 16, 17, 20, 36, 57, 59
Mississippi State Historical Museum, 39-40
Mississippi Territory, 17, 58
Moon Lake, 8
Museum of Natural History, 42
music, 45-48
Nanih Waiya Mound, 40-41
Nashville, Tennessee, 17
Natchez, 11, 16, 17, 36, 54, 56, 58
Natchez people, 14, 16
Natchez Trace, **8,** 17, **17**
Netter, Mildrette, 55
Nicholson, Eliza Poitevent Holbrook (Pearl Rivers), 48

nicknames, Mississippi's, 4, 24, 54, 56
Ocean Springs, 16, 32-33
Old Spanish Fort, 32
Oxford, 42, 58
Pascagoula, 23, 32, 54, 57
Pascagoula people, 14
Pascagoula River, 8, 32, 57
Payne Field, 22
Payton, Walter, 52, **52**
Pearl River, **6,** 8, 57
Perry, Harold, 35
Philadelphia, 24, 59
Pickwick Lake, 57
Piggtown, 55
Piney Woods, 9
plantations, 18, **18,** 22, **35,** 36-37, **37,** 41
population, 17, 27, 39, 57, 59
Port Gibson, **17**
Presley, Elvis, 43, **46,** 47-48
Price, Leontyne, 45-46, **45**
Pride, Charlie, 48
Revels, Hiram Rhoades, 20-21
Rice, Jerry, 52
rivers, 7-8, 57
Rivers, Pearl, 48
Robards, Rachel, 37
Robertson Museum, 40
Rodgers, Jimmie, Museum, 40
Rosalie, 36
Rosemont Plantation, 36
Ross Barnett Lake, 8, 57
Rowan Oak, 42, **43, 49**
Sardis Lake, 57
Scranton Floating Museum, 32
Seafood Industry Museum, 33
sharecroppers, 22, **22**
shipbuilding, 23, 27
Ship Island, 7, 34, 55

slavery, 16, 18-19, **18,** 20, 58
Spanish, 17, 58
sports, 51-52, **51,** 55
Springfield Plantation, 36-37, **37**
state symbols, 9, 10, 56-57, **56, 57**
Stennis Space Center, 28
Still, William Grant, 45
Sunflower, 55
Tallahatchie River, 8, 57
Taylor, Mildred, 51
Tennessee-Tombigbee Waterway, 59
Tombigbee River, 57
topography, 7-8, **8**
tourism, 4, 25, 28, 32
Tupelo, 43, 57
USS *Cairo* Museum, 38, **38**
Van Dorn, Earl, 43
Vaughan, 54
Vicksburg, 4, **12-13,** 19-20, **19, 25,** 38-39, **38,** 58
Walker, Charles, 55
Washington, 56
Washington Lake, 8
Waters, Muddy, 47, **47**
Welty, Eudora, 50
White, Willye, 55
wildlife, 9-10, **9, 10,** 33, 34, 35, 55, 57
Williams, Thomas Lanier, **50,** 51
Windsor, 37, **37**
Winfrey, Oprah, 52-53, **52**
Winterville Mounds, 41
Woodall Mountain, 7, 56
Woodville, 35, 36
World War I, 22, 59
World War II, 23, 59
Wright, Richard, 50, **50**
Yazoo City, 54
Yazoo people, 14
Yazoo River, 8, 38, 57

ABOUT THE AUTHORS

Dennis and Judith Fradin have coauthored several books in the From Sea to Shining Sea series. The Fradins both graduated from Northwestern University in 1967. Dennis has been a professional writer for twenty years, and has published 150 books. His works for Childrens Press include the Young People's Stories of Our States series, the Disaster! series, and the Thirteen Colonies series. Judith earned her M.A. in literature from Northwestern University and taught high-school and college English for many years. The Fradins, who are the parents of Anthony, Diana, and Michael, live in Evanston, Illinois.